Sex, Money & Sp

QUOTATIONS
ON THE ONLY TH
MEN ~~CARE~~ *talk* ABC

COMPILED BY

MICHAEL MA

PRENTICE HALL PR

I really didn't say everything I said.

YOGI BERRA

To David

my son, my friend, my pupil, my teacher

Contents

Money

Sports

Introduction

As Dale Berra said, comparing himself to his famous father, Yogi Berra, "Our similarities are different." That's how I feel about these three distinct topics— sex, money, and sports. They're different yet somehow they fit together. What they have in common is the abiding interest men have in them. Just about every man has experienced both the agony and the ecstasy of sex; just about every man has had enough money at some time in his life, and he has also been broke; and just about every man has been involved in sports and has experienced the joy of winning and the heartbreak of defeat.

At the same time, I find that each topic has its own character. At the mere mention of sex, people are ready to laugh. It is no surprise, then, that most of the things men say about sex are humorous. We're still maturing about sex (meaning we don't understand anything about it), so we're not very willing to talk about a serious sexual matter with friends the way we would if we were discussing a football game. No, we're still pretty reserved, so humor is our best and safest route. Besides, it's a lot of fun to laugh about sex.

Money is a serious matter, however. Most of the quotes I found about money were serious and belonged in college business textbooks. But I found other quotes, ranging from funny to serious, from philosophical to flippant, from truthful to silly, that seem to touch a part of all of us. After all, a good chunk of our lives is spent hassling with money issues, no matter how much or how little we have. So, the best approach to money is one that is both humorous and serious.

Sports is another thing altogether. Here we find reverence, not unlike a religion. Men love their sports. Why? For many reasons. Sports are big-time hobbies for men, whether they're playing or watching. Men's heroes—and boys' heroes—are athletes. Men are nurtured by sports since sports often take place outdoors, sometimes in stunning places, like fishing in a gorgeous mountain stream. Men like nothing better than a Monday Night Football party. Sports provide a metaphor for men's daily lives, especially the winning and losing part. Sports also provide an outlet for men's otherwise pent-up cave-man tendencies.

Men say such affectionate things about sports. And they say such hilarious things—about themselves, others, and their beloved sports. The sports quotes in this book are funny, loving, self-deprecating, insightful, quirky, and sometimes even serious—pretty much the way most men think of sports.

Last, I point out the obvious: that men are interested not only in sex, money, and sports, but also in other topics, such as politics, religion, education, and jobs, to name a few. But of all the areas of interest men may share, these three seem to be the ones they talk most about—the most common denominator. And to give that common denominator a little more precision, I have chosen to quote *only* men on these topics in order to see specifically what men have to say about them. Of course, men's opinions on these topics can be of as much interest to women as men. This book, then, is for both men and women who want to know and enjoy what men have to say about sex, money, and sports.

SEX

DATING

I'm dating a woman now who, evidently, is unaware
of it.

GARY SHANDLING

I was on a date. I was really uncomfortable. My guts
were churning—it was really awkward. So finally,
I figured, hey, I'll just ask her, "What's your name?"

STEVE BRIDGES

I'm driving her home all right, and that's when I start to wonder if there's going to be any sex—and if I'm gonna be involved.

GARRY SHANDLING

One woman I was dating said, "Come on over, there's nobody home." I went over—nobody was home.

RODNEY DANGERFIELD

The weird names they have for automobiles these days! How do you get a woman to sit in a Ford Probe for the first time?"

JAY LENO

I go from stool to stool in singles bars hoping to get lucky, but there's never any gum under any of them.

EMO PHILLIPS

I'm not very romantic. I was with my girlfriend at a restaurant. A man at the table next to us was saying, "Pass the honey, honey." His female companion said, "Pass the sugar, sugar." I turned to my girlfriend and said, "Pass the tea. . .bag."

SCOTT WOOD

I have no self-confidence. When girls tell me yes, I tell them to think it over.

RODNEY DANGERFIELD

I just broke up with someone and the last thing she said to me was, "You'll never find anyone like me again!" I'm thinking, "I should hope not! If I don't want you, why would I want someone like you?"

LARRY MILLER

Let's face it, a date is like a job interview that lasts all night. The only difference between the two is that there are very few job interviews where there's a chance you will end up naked at the end of it.

JERRY SEINFELD

MAKIN' WHOOPEE

Anybody who believes that the way to a man's heart is through his stomach flunked geography.

ROBERT BYRNE

If I don't do it every day, I get a headache.

WILLIE NELSON

It's okay to laugh in the bedroom so long as you don't point.

WILL DURST

I practice safe sex. I use an airbag. It's a little startling at first when it flies out. Then the woman realizes it's safer than being thrown clear.

GARRY SHANDLING

She was a lovely girl. Our courtship was fast and furious: I was fast and she was furious.

MAX KAUFFMANN

Seems to me the basic conflict between men and women, sexually, is that men are like firemen. To us, sex is an emergency, and no matter what we're doing we can be ready in two minutes. Women, on the other hand, are like fire. They're very exciting, but the conditions have to be exactly right for it to occur.

JERRY SEINFELD

Music helps set a romantic mood. Some men believe the only good music is live music. Imagine her surprise when you say. "I don't need a stereo—I have an accordion!" Then imagine the sound of the door slamming.

MARTIN MULL

Warning signs that your lover is bored: 1. Passionless kisses; 2. Frequent sighing; 3. Moved, left no forwarding address.

MATT GROENING

Sexual intercourse is like having someone else blow your nose.

PHILIP LARKIN

Love is 2 minutes 52 seconds of squishing noises. It shows your mind isn't clicking right.

JOHNNY ROTTEN

Whoever named it necking was a poor judge
of anatomy.

GROUCHO MARX

He moved his lips about her ears and neck as though
in thirsting search of an erogenous zone. A waste of
time, he knew from experience. Erogenous zones were
either everywhere or nowhere.

JOSEPH HELLER

After making love I said to my girl, "Was it good for
you, too?" And she said, "I don't think this was good
for anybody."

GARRY SHANDLING

During sex I fantasize that I'm someone else.

RICHARD LEWIS

Last time I tried to make love to my wife nothing was happening, so I said to her, "What's the matter, you can't think of anybody either?"

RODNEY DANGERFIELD

Politically incorrect T-shirt idea: What part of "AWW C'MON, PLEASE?" don't you understand?

ROGER CREW

It's very awkward being a single guy with all the diseases around. You know, it's to the point where I won't go to bed with a woman unless she says, "All right, I'll go to bed with you."

GARRY SHANDLING

The most romantic thing any woman ever said to me in bed was, "Are you sure you're not a cop?"

LARRY BROWN

The reason people sweat is so they won't catch fire when making love.

DON ROSE

Sex is good, but not as good as fresh sweet corn.

GARRISON KEILLOR

The only people who make love all the time are liars.

TELLY SAVALAS

You gotta learn that if you don't get it by midnight, chances are you ain't gonna get it; and if you do, it ain't worth it.

CASEY STENGEL

Once, while we were making love, a curious optical illusion occurred, and it almost looked as though she were moving.

WOODY ALLEN

When two people make love, there are at least four people present—the two who are actually there and the two they are thinking about.

SIGMUND FREUD

My schoolmates would make love to anything that moved, but I never saw any reason to limit myself.

EMO PHILLIPS

The first time we ever made love I said, "Am I the first man that ever made love to you?" She said, "You could be. You look damn familiar."

RONNIE BULLARD

Low self-esteem sex is bad. When I have an orgasm, I shriek, "I'm sorry!"

RICHARD LEWIS

I'm getting old. When I squeeze into a tight parking space, I'm sexually satisfied for the day.

RODNEY DANGERFIELD

Contraceptives should be used on all conceivable occasions.

SPIKE MILLIGAN

I want to tell you a terrific story about oral contraception. I asked this girl to sleep with me and she said "No."

WOODY ALLEN

For birth control I rely on my personality.

MILT ABEL

Some condoms are made of sheep intestines, but I was so scared the first time I wore the whole sheep.

DANNY WILLIAMS

Some people say, "Gee, well, making love and wearing a condom is like taking a shower and wearing a raincoat." Maybe, but these days, making love and not wearing a condom is like taking a shower and wearing a toaster.

MARK PRICE

An adult western is where the hero still kisses his horse at the end only now he worries about it.

MILTON BERLE

We did one of those quick, awkward kisses where each one of you gets a nose in the eye.

CLIVE JAMES

I get very sexually excited on stage. It's like making love to 9,000 people at once.

PRINCE

The first girl you go to bed with is always pretty.

WALTER MATHAU

I told my girlfriend that unless she expressed her feelings and told me what she liked I wouldn't be able to please her, so she said, "Get off me."

GARRY SHANDLING

Are you about average? The average orgasm·is only 10 seconds long. The average frequency of intercourse is once or twice a week. That's 20 seconds a week, one and a half minutes a month, 18 minutes a year. In 50 years that's about 15 hours. For 15 hours of ecstasy, we devote how many thousands and thousands of hours to thinking about sex, worrying about sex, day-dreaming about sex, wishing for sex, planning for sex?

ALAN BAUER

I once made love for an hour and fifteen minutes, but it was the night the clocks are set ahead.

GARRY SHANDLING

It's the most fun I ever had without laughing.

WOODY ALLEN

SOLO SEX

Masturbation is the thinking man's television.

CHRISTOPHER HAMPTON

Homer, in the second book of the *Illiad*, says with fine enthusiasm, "Give me masturbation or give me death!"

MARK TWAIN

What I like about masturbation is that you don't have to talk afterwards.

MILOS FORMAN

I was the best I ever had.

WOODY ALLEN

Many mothers are wholly ignorant of the almost universal prevalence of secret vice, or self-abuse, among the young. Why hesitate to say firmly and without quibble that personal abuse lies at the root of much of the feebleness, paleness, nervousness, and good-for-nothingness of the entire community.

DR. J.H. KELLOGG

The good thing about masturbation is that you don't have to dress up for it.

TRUMAN CAPOTE

The only reason I feel so guilty about masturbation is that I do it so badly.

DAVID STEINBERG

Shaking hands with the unemployed.

GEORGE CARLIN

Self-abuse is the devil's telephone booth.

EDWARD BARKER

If God had intended us not to masturbate, He would have made our arms shorter.

GEORGE CARLIN

Father: You keep [masturbating] and you'll go blind. Son: Then I'll just do it until I need glasses.

JOHN BONI

THE MAGIC WAND

Women think men are led around by their penises. We're not. It points us in a direction, I'll give you that.

GARRY SHANDLING

Women say it's not how much men have, but what we do with it. How many things can we do with it? What is it, a Cuisinart? It's got two speeds: forward and reverse.

RICHARD JENI

Car profiles gave me erections, sports statistics gave me erections, the topology of hillsides gave me erections, and so did dogs, cats, bears, deer, several species of birds, and one or two tree species. That's what it's like to be a young male.

BRIAN FAWCETT

Don't forget, the penis is mightier than the sword.

SCREAMIN' JAY HAWKINS

An erection at will is the moral equivalent of a valid credit card.

ALEX COMFORT

[An erection] hinges on the general well-being of the body—a head cold, hangnail, indigestion, money worries, anything, and you can kiss your erection good-bye.

JOHN BONI

Science magazine came out with a report on the difference between men's and women's brains. Apparently women are more controlled by a part of the brain called singletgyrus, and men are more controlled by a part of the brain known as the penis.

JAY LENO

I said to my doctor the other day, "My penis is burning." He said, "That's just because someone is talking about it."

GARRY SHANDLING

My mother is Welsh, my father is Hungarian—which makes me Wel-Hung.

BILLY RIBACK

Stand back, honey. I don't know how big this thing is going to get.

ADAM TO EVE

Sometimes a cigar is just a cigar.

SIGMUND FREUD

LOVE

Never forget that the most powerful force on earth is love.

NELSON ROCKEFELLER

Love is the greatest refreshment in life.

PABLO PICASSO

One is very crazy when in love.

SIGMUND FREUD

If two people love each other, there can be no happy
end to it.

ERNEST HEMINGWAY

Everything we do in life is based on fear,
especially love.

MEL BROOKS

Love is the self-delusion we manufacture to justify
the trouble we take to have sex.

DAN GREENBURG

The difference between sex and love is that sex
relieves tension and love causes it.

WOODY ALLEN

Sex without love is an empty experience, but, as
empty experiences go, it's one of the best.

WOODY ALLEN

I love Mickey Mouse more than any woman I've
ever known.

WALT DISNEY

Ah, love—the walks over soft grass, the smiles over candlelight, the arguments over just about everything else.

MAX HEADROOM

It's an extra dividend when you like the girl you're in love with.

CLARK GABLE

Things are just too sophisticated out there in L.A. If guys fall in love, they think they have to buy wine and candy and roses. Hell, in the South, when we fall in love, we just spray-paint your name on an overpass.

JEFF FOXWORTHY

Send two dozen roses to room 424 and put "Emily, I love you" on the back of the bill.

GROUCHO MARX

The most important things to do in this world are to get something to eat, something to drink and somebody to love you.

BRENDAN BEHAN

Love is an obsessive delusion that is cured by marriage.

KARL BOWMAN

Tying the Knot

Marriage should be a duet: when one sings, the other claps.

JOE MURRAY

A happy home is one in which each spouse grants the possibility that the other may be right, though neither believes it.

DON FRASER

I have learned that only two things are necessary to keep one's wife happy. First, let her think she's having her way. And second, let her have it.

LYNDON B. JOHNSON

Marriage is an alliance entered into by a man who can't sleep with the window shut, and a woman who can't sleep with the window open.

GEORGE BERNARD SHAW

It's a funny thing that when a man hasn't anything on earth to worry about, he goes off and gets married.

ROBERT FROST

I've been married to the same woman for fourteen years, which is like eighty-something in L.A. years.

ROBERT G. LEE

We sleep in separate rooms, we have dinner apart, we take separate vacations—we're doing everything we can to keep our marriage together.

RODNEY DANGERFIELD

Some people ask the secret of our long marriage. We take time to go to a restaurant two times a week. A little candlelight dinner, soft music and dancing. She goes Tuesdays, I go Fridays.

HENNY YOUNGMAN

The other night I said to my wife, Ruth, "Do you feel that the sex and excitement has gone out of our marriage?" Ruth said, "I'll discuss it with you during the next commercial."

MILTON BERLE

My wife and I have been together so long, I know we'll never break up. Yes, there's love and commitment, but the main reason we'll always be together is that neither one of us can imagine having to retrain somebody new.

ROBERT G. LEE

Keep your eyes wide open before marriage, half shut afterward.

BENJAMIN FRANKLIN

The first part of our marriage was very happy. But then, on the way back from the ceremony. . .

HENNY YOUNGMAN

Where I come from, when a Catholic marries a Lutheran it is considered the first step on the road to Minneapolis.

GARRISON KEILLOR

If Americans throw rice at weddings, do Chinese throw hot dogs?

LARRY ANDERSEN

The bride wears white to symbolize purity. The groom wears black.

DAVID FROST

The groom's party should wear pastel senior-prom-style outfits rented at the shopping mall. The bride's party should wear expensive dresses so unattractive that they can never be used again, even as tourniquets.

DAVE BARRY

Left up to the grooms of the world (which it isn't and never will be), weddings would be come-as-you-are, three-minute rituals held in auto-part stores.

J. JORDAN CANNADY

You ever go to a wedding where you know the marriage isn't going to last? You don't want to say anything, but you don't want to spend a hundred bucks on a gift either. It's a dilemma. "Here's a lottery ticket. Good luck to you."

MARK FARRELL

Eventually in your life, you have to get married. You just have to. That's probably what I'll say at the ceremony. I'll go, "I have to."

GARRY SHANDLING

My wife and I were happy for twenty years. Then we met.

RODNEY DANGERFIELD

My parents stayed together for forty years, but that was out of spite.

WOODY ALLEN

Marriage is really tough because you have to deal with feelings and lawyers.

RICHARD PRYOR

I don't think I'll get married again. I'll just find a woman I don't like and give her a house.

LEWIS GRIZZARD

We were happily married for eight months. Unfortunately we were married for four and a half years.

NICK FALDO

Always get married early in the morning. That way, if it doesn't work out, you haven't wasted a whole day.

MICKEY ROONEY

Do you know what it means to come home at night to a woman who'll give you a little love, a little affection, a little tenderness? It means you're in the wrong house, that's what it means.

GEORGE BURNS

A man's friends like him but leave him as he is—his wife loves him and is always trying to turn him into somebody else.

G.K. CHESTERTON

I never knew what real happiness was until I got married. And by then it was too late.

MAX KAUFFMANN

The concept of two people living together for twenty-five years without having a cross word suggests a lack of spirit only to be admired in sheep.

A.P. HERBERT

It destroys one's nerves to be amiable every day to the same human being.

BENJAMIN DISRAELI

Sex in marriage is like medicine. Three times a day for the first week. Then once a day for another week. Then once every three or four days until the condition clears up.

PETER DE VRIES

What do I know about sex? I'm a married man.

TOM CLANCY

Sex drive: A physical craving that begins in adolescence and ends at marriage.

ROBERT BYRNE

Marriage is like a bank account. You put it in, you take it out, you lose interest.

IRWIN COREY

We would have broken up except for the children. Who were the children? Well, she and I were.

MORT SAHL

Marriage, as far as I'm concerned, is one of the most wonderful, heartwarming, satisfying experiences a human can have. I've only been married seventeen years, so I haven't seen that side of it yet.

GEORGE GOBEL

Marriage is a lot like the army: everyone complains, but you'd be surprised at the large number that re-enlist.

JAMES GARNER

Marriage is not a man's idea. A woman must have thought of it. Years ago some guy said, "Let me get this straight, honey. I can't sleep with anyone else for the rest of my life, and if things don't work out, you get to keep half of my stuff? What a great idea."

BOBBY SLAYTON

The tragedy of marriage is that while all women marry thinking that their man will change, all men marry believing their wives will never change. Both are invariably disappointed.

BERNIE SAMPSON

If you want to grow up real quick, get married.

MIKE TYSON

Being married reduces the chance of a heart attack, or anything exciting.

JONATHAN KATZ

If variety is the spice of life, marriage is the big can of leftover Spam.

JOHNNY CARSON

The only difference about being married is that you don't have to get out of bed to fart.

JIMMY GOLDSMITH

A friend of mine got married and called. He said, "My wife pays more attention to the baby than me." I said, "It seems to me you've got to understand: The baby is blood relations to your wife. That's her son. You're some guy she met in a bar. She knows it, the kid knows it, and I'm sure they have a good laugh about it when you are at work."

GARRY SHANDLING

I love being married. I was single for a long time and I just got sick of finishing my own sentences.

BRIAN KILEY

[Once you're married], you lose the ability to get dressed for yourself.

PAUL REISER

Being married or single is a choice we all have to make. It's not a great choice. . . . It's sort of like when the doctor goes, "Ointment or suppositories?"

RICHARD JENI

I don't think it would be a bad idea if we dissolved the whole idea of marriage. I think possibly we'd end up doing the same things we're doing now anyway.

BURT REYNOLDS

There are no successful marriages. There are only those that are succeeding—or failing.

WELLS GOODRICH

In every marriage more than a week old, there are grounds for divorce. The trick is to find, and continue to find, grounds for marriage.

ROBERT ANDERSON

There is no more lovely, friendly or charming relationship, communion or company, than a good marriage.

MARTIN LUTHER

Small Fries

Having children is like having a bowling alley installed in your brain.

MARTIN MULL

To enter life by way of the vagina is as good a
way as any.

HENRY MILLER

Never date a woman you can hear ticking.

MARK PATINKIN

Boy, parents—there's a tough job. Damn easy job to
get, though. I think most people love the interview.
You don't have to dress for it.

STEVE BRUNER

We've been trying to have a kid. Well, she was trying.
I just laid there.

BOB SAGET

I think any guy who films his wife giving birth, she ought to be able to film his hemorrhoid surgery later on. "Look girls, Tony is totally dilated. What a trouper he was!"

JEFF FOXWORTHY

I was Cesarean born. You can't really tell, although whenever I leave a house, I go out through a window.

STEVEN WRIGHT

I can't believe that out of 100,000 sperm, you were the quickest.

STEVEN PEARL

A baby is an inestimable blessing and a bother.

MARK TWAIN

If you were to open up a baby's head—and I am not suggesting for a moment that you should—you would find nothing but an enormous drool gland.

DAVE BARRY

She's in the crib with one part of the intercom and I'm in the other room. "Breaker one-nine, Daddy, I got spit-up on my shirt and I'm packing a load. Please come in and help me."

BOB SAGET

My mother loved children—she would have given anything if I had been one.

GROUCHO MARX

When I was a kid my parents moved a lot, but I always found them.

RODNEY DANGERFIELD

We had a quicksand box in our backyard. I was an only child—eventually.

STEVEN WRIGHT

When I was kidnapped, my parents snapped into action. They rented out my room.

WOODY ALLEN

I can be President of the United States or I can control Alice. I cannot possibly do both.

THEODORE ROOSEVELT

My father used to tell me, "When Abraham Lincoln was your age, Abraham Lincoln had a job. When Abraham Lincoln was your age, he walked twelve miles to get to school." I said, "Dad, when Abraham Lincoln was your age, he was President, okay?"

ANDY ANDREWS

I'm amazed how much little boys are like poltergeists: You don't see them do it, but they'll stand in the middle of a room—one little boy—and there'll be noise from everywhere, things flying off shelves—and you don't know how they do it.

DAVE BARRY

When I was a kid I said to my father one afternoon, "Daddy, will you take me to the zoo?" He answered, "If the zoo wants you, let them come and get you."

JERRY LEWIS

For years I thought I was adopted. Until one day I just got bold. I went up to my dad and asked him straight out. I said, "Ling Chow. . ."

SCOTT WOOD

The thing that impresses me most about America is the way parents obey their children.

EDWARD VIII, DUKE OF WINDSOR

The value of marriage is not that adults produce children, but that children produce adults.

PETER DE VRIES

Children are the living message we send to a time we will not see.

JOHN W. WHITEHEAD

Affairs

If I'm not in bed by eleven at night, I go home.

HENNY YOUNGMAN

There is one thing I would break up over, and that is if she caught me with another woman. I won't stand for that.

STEVE MARTIN

I've been in love with the same woman for forty-one years. If my wife finds out, she'll kill me.

HENNY YOUNGMAN

My mother-in-law broke up my marriage. One day my wife came home early from work and found us in bed together.

LENNY BRUCE

Monogamous is what one partner in every relationship wants to be.

STRANGE DE JIM

A man can have two, maybe three love affairs while he's married. After that it's cheating.

YVES MONTAND

Here's to our wives and sweethearts—may they
never meet.

JOHN BUNNY

The big difference between sex for money and sex for
free is that sex for money usually costs less.

BRENDAN BEHAN

If I had as many love affairs as you have given me
credit for, I would now be speaking to you from a jar
in the Harvard Medical School.

FRANK SINATRA

I walked in on my wife and the milkman, the first
thing she said is, "Don't tell the butcher!"

RODNEY DANGERFIELD

There was a girl knocking on my hotel room door all night last night. I finally had to let her out of my room.

HENNY YOUNGMAN

President Clinton celebrated his nineteenth wedding anniversary this year. Bill said he celebrated with a romantic dinner for two and a night in a fancy hotel. Hillary said she just saw a movie.

JON STEWART

If you're going to do something tonight that you'll be sorry for tomorrow—sleep late.

HENNY YOUNGMAN

A man does not look behind the doors unless he has been there himself.

HENRI DU BOIS

Just 'cause you look at another woman, it doesn't mean you are going to do anything. I mean, you are at a restaurant and food comes to another table, you might look at it. It doesn't mean you are gonna dive in and start eating it. It's not like I look at another woman and turn to my girlfriend and say, "I wish I got that. Why didn't I get what he's having?"

GARRY SHANDLING

Untying the Knot

Our parents got divorced when we were kids and it was kind of cool. We got to go to divorce court with them. It was like a game show. My mom won the house and car. We're all excited. My dad got some luggage.

TOM ARNOLD

She cried, and the judge wiped her tears with my checkbook.

TOMMY MANVILLE

Three of my wives were very good housekeepers. After we got divorced, they kept the house.

WILLIE PEP

You never realize how short a month is until you pay alimony.

JOHN BARRYMORE

Ah, yes, divorce, from the Latin word meaning to rip out a man's genitals through his wallet.

ROBIN WILLIAMS

Divorce: Termination of a marriage before either spouse can terminate the other. According to custom, both parties enter into a knockdown legal battle that is always won by their attorneys and usually lost by their children.

RICK BAYAN

My divorce came as a complete surprise to me.
That will happen when you haven't been home in
eighteen years.

LEE TREVINO

Many a man owes his success to his first wife and his
second wife to his success.

JIM BACKUS

The worst thing to do during a separation is to go
through your photo albums. They're just full of great
memories: vacations, birthdays, Christmas. I guess
that's 'cause we never take photographs of lousy
moments we share together. Next time you're having
a fight, stop for a snapshot.

BRENT BIASKOSKI

Lisa Marie has filed for divorce. According to her attorney she's going to make [Michael Jackson] pay through the noses.

CONAN O'BRIEN

Julia Roberts and Lyle Lovett broke up this week. Roberts says that her marriage was over when she realized, "I'm Julia Roberts and he's Lyle Lovett."

NORM MACDONALD

When a couple decides to divorce, they should inform both sets of parents before having a party and telling all their friends. This is not only courteous but practical. Parents may be very willing to pitch in with comments, criticism and malicious gossip of their own to help the divorce along.

P.J. O'ROURKE

My first wife divorced me on grounds of incompatibility—and besides, I think she hated me.

OSCAR LEVANT

Divorces are sometimes caused by husbands having dinner with their secretaries, but more often by having breakfast with their wives.

A.P. HERBERT

More marriages have been ruined by irritating habits than by unfaithfulness.

H.R.L. SHEPPARD

I couldn't see tying myself down to a middle-aged woman with four children, even though the woman was my wife and the children were my own.

JOSEPH HELLER

It wasn't exactly a divorce—I was traded.

TIM CONWAY

On the Wild Side

I'm not kinky, but occasionally I like to put on a robe and stand in front of a tennis ball machine.

GARRY SHANDLING

I don't know if you've ever had a woman eat an apple while you were doing it. . . . Well, you can imagine how that affects you.

HENRY MILLER

What a man enjoys about a woman's clothes are his fantasies of how she would look without them.

BRENDAN FRANCIS

Girls are always running through my mind. They don't dare walk.

ANDY GIBB

I'm too shy to express my sexual needs except over the phone to people I don't know.

GARRY SHANDLING

Sex means spank and beautiful means bottom and always will.

KENNETH TYNAN

Kinky sex involves the use of duck feathers. Perverted sex involves the whole duck.

LEWIS GRIZZARD

You sofa-crevice fondler!

PETER DE VRIES

Is sex dirty? Only if it's done right.

WOODY ALLEN

I'm all for bringing back the birch, but only between consenting adults.

GORE VIDAL

If it weren't for pickpockets, I'd have no sex life at all.

RODNEY DANGERFIELD

It is very disturbing indeed when you can't think of any new perversions that you would like to practice.

JAMES DICKEY

She was so wild that when she made French toast she got her tongue caught in the toaster.

RODNEY DANGERFIELD

Get in good physical condition before submitting to bondage. You should be fit to be tied.

ROBERT BYRNE

The only unnatural sex act is that which you cannot perform.

ALFRED KINSEY

Ever try to make love in a kayak?

LEWIS GRIZZARD

When I'm in a wig I'm pretty attractive. I stare at myself in mirrors because I'm my type.

KEVIN MCDONALD

I've been to [*Victoria's Secret*] a few times. I'll give you guys a tip: Establish that you're not there looking for something in your size right off.

ROSS SCHAEFFER

You know what's fun to do? Rent an adult movie, take it home, record over it with *The Wizard of Oz*, then return it so the next guy that rents it is thinking, "When is this Dorothy chick going to get naked?"

MARK PITTA

Sex between a man and a woman can be wonderful—provided you get between the right man and the right woman.

WOODY ALLEN

You get a better class of person at orgies, because people have to keep in trim more. There is an awful lot of going around holding in your stomach, you know. Everybody is very polite to each other. The conversation isn't very good, but you can't have everything.

GORE VIDAL

I believe sex is a beautiful thing between two people. Between five, it's fantastic.

WOODY ALLEN

Ménage à trois is a French term. It means
"Kodak moment."

GREG RAY

A survey asking men who they would want to be
stranded with on a desert island has Pamela Anderson
tied with Sharon Stone. Of course, the number-one
choice was Pamela Anderson tied *to* Sharon Stone.

CONAN O'BRIEN

I'm not *against* naked girls—not as often as I'd
like to be.

BENNY HILL

A reporter who visited a nudist camp asked one of
the campers, "How did you get to be a nudist?" The
camper replied, "I was born that way."

LEONARD LYONS

The citizens' committee to clean up New York's porn-infested areas continued its series of rallies today, as a huge, throbbing, pulsating crowd sprang erect from nowhere and forced its way into the steaming nether regions surrounding the glistening, sweating intersection of Eighth Avenue and Forty-Second Street. Thrusting, driving, pushing its way into the usually receptive neighborhood, the excited throng, now grown to five times its original size, rammed itself again and again and again into the quivering, perspiring, musty dankness, fluctuating between eager anticipation and trembling revulsion. Now suddenly the tumescent crowd and the irresistible area were one heaving, alternately melting and thawing turgid entity, ascending to heights heretofore unexperienced. Then, with a gigantic, soul-searching, heart-stopping series of eruptions, it was over. Afterwards, the crowd had a cigarette and went home.

SATURDAY NIGHT LIVE

VENUS

Of all the wild beasts of land or sea, the wildest is woman.

MEANDER

Someone once asked Mark Twain, "In a world without women, what would men become?" He replied, "Scarce, sir, mighty scarce."

MARK TWAIN

As for evolution, I have a hard time believing that billions of years ago two protozoa bumped into each other under a volcanic cesspool and evolved into Cindy Crawford.

ROBERT G. LEE

There are no ugly women; there are only women who do not know how to look pretty.

JEAN DE LA BRUYÈRE

Her face was her chaperone.

RUPERT HUGHES

I like a woman with a head on her shoulders.
I hate necks.

STEVE MARTIN

My wife has a whim of iron.

OLIVER HERFORD

Women would rather be right than reasonable.

OGDEN NASH

Ten measures of speech descended on the world;
women took nine and men one.

THE TALMUD

A woman in love will do almost anything for a man,
except give up the desire to improve him.

NATHANIEL BRANDEN

For a man, getting dressed up is anything that
requires underwear and socks. Whereas a woman gets
her hair done, puts on makeup, tummy toner, a short
skirt, and high heels, then says she wants to "find a
man who loves me for *me*!"

ROBERT G. LEE

Men may deny it, but I think their motivation to succeed, to be incredibly powerful and opulent and to maintain an overwhelming, titanic status in the community is for women. It is a sexual thing—it's done for either hands-on gratification or for the sexual allure. Power. That's what women are drawn to.

SYLVESTER STALLONE

Women are not the weak, frail little flowers that they are advertised. There has never been anything invented yet, including war, that man would enter into, that a woman wouldn't, too.

WILL ROGERS

Never ask a woman why she's angry at you. She'll either get angrier at you for not knowing, or she'll tell you. Both ways, you lose.

IAN SHOALES

The way to fight a woman is with your hat. Grab it and run.

JOHN BARRYMORE

Only choose in marriage a woman whom you would choose as a friend if she were a man.

JOSEPH JOUBERT

Women are smarter than men because they listen.

PHIL DONAHUE

I hate women because they always know where things are.

JAMES THURBER

For women shopping is a sport, much like deer hunting is to men. They are building a new mall in my town. Last week, women were hanging on the fence yelling at the workmen for taking a lunch break.

JEFF FOXWORTHY

If a woman has to choose between catching a fly ball and saving an infant's life, she will choose to save the infant's life without even considering if there are men on base.

DAVE BARRY

Have you heard of this new book entitled *1,001 Sex Secrets Men Should Know*? It contains comments from 1,001 women on how men can be better in bed. I think that women would actually settle for three: Slow down, turn off the TV, call out the right name.

JAY LENO

Despite my thirty years of research into the feminine soul, I have not yet been able to answer. . .the great question that has never been answered: What does a woman want?

SIGMUND FREUD

MARS

There are two things no man will admit he can't do well: drive and make love.

STIRLING MOSS

The bravest thing that men do is love women.

MORT SAHL

To women, we are like big dogs that talk.

LARRY MILLER

Men aren't men until they can get to Sears
by themselves.

TIM ALLEN

The average male thinks about sex every 11 minutes
while he's awake.

PATRICK GREENE

Males cannot look at breasts and think at the
same time.

DAVE BARRY

Men are superior to women. For one thing, they can urinate from a speeding car.

WILL DURST

Men have lost touch with their Spears, their Maces, their Battering Rams, and what have they replaced them with? Weed Eaters.

JOE BOB BRIGGS

Male sexual response is far brisker and more automatic. It is triggered easily by things—like putting a quarter in a vending machine.

ALEX COMFORT

It's everywhere you look now. You can't even go to the bookstore anymore. All the books got the same title—*Good Women, Bad Men*. Watch any afternoon talk show—"Why men don't deserve to live, next on Donahue." Pick up a woman's magazine, look at the articles inside—"The Penis: Sex Organ or Birth Defect?"

ROB BECKER

Basically my wife was immature. I'd be at home in the bath and she'd come in and sink my boats.

WOODY ALLEN

Only a man would take time out of his busy schedule to light a fart. There's not a man in this room who hasn't seen it, heard about it, or done it himself.

TIM ALLEN

In their efforts to find their inner child, lost father, or car keys, white males need to go way back. In fact, they need to travel back to the moment when Christopher Columbus landed in America, fell to his knees on the sand and said, "But my mother never loved me."

SHERMAN ALEXIE

My wife thinks I'm too nosy. At least that's what she keeps scribbling in her diary.

DRAKE SATHER

I'd like to go to an assertiveness-training class. First I need to check with my wife.

ADAM CHRISTING

The sure way to tell if a man is a bachelor is to check his silverware. If it's full of nicks from going through the garbage disposal a couple of dozen times, he's for real.

NICK ARNETTE

Men and women both care about smell, but women go to the trouble to smell good. Men are like, "Does this stink too bad to wear one more time? Maybe I should iron it."

JEFF FOXWORTHY

In the last couple of weeks I have seen ads for the Wonder Bra. Is that really a problem in this country? Men not paying enough attention to women's breasts?

JAY LENO

THE LAST WORD

The mirror over my bed reads: Objects appear larger than they are.

GARRY SHANDLING

Condoms aren't completely safe. A friend of mine was wearing one and got hit by a bus.

BOB RUBIN

I wasn't kissing her, I was whispering in her mouth.

CHICO MARX

Sex after ninety is like trying to shoot pool with a rope. Even putting my cigar in its holder is a thrill.

GEORGE BURNS

In the case of some women, orgasms take a bit of time. Before signing on with a partner, make sure you are willing to lay aside, say, the month of June, with sandwiches having to be brought in.

BRUCE JAY FRIEDMAN

I dated this girl for two years—and then the nagging starts: "I wanna know your name."

MIKE BINDER

I'm very loyal in a relationship. Any relationship. When I go out with my mom, I don't look at other moms. I don't go, "Oooooh, I wonder what her macaroni and cheese tastes like."

GARRY SHANDLING

I was at one wedding and the priest was skeptical. You know that part where he has to say, "If anyone can show why these two people should not be together"? He goes, "Then please line up behind the microphone I set up and I'll try to get to as many of you as I can before lunch."

MARK FARRELL

I have an intense desire to return to the womb. Anybody's.

WOODY ALLEN

I lost my parents at the beach when I was a kid. I asked a lifeguard to help me find them. He said, "I don't know, kid, there are so many places they could hide."

RODNEY DANGERFIELD

I live alone. I'm not married. I hope to be someday so I can stop exercising.

JEFF STILTON

Oysters are supposed to enhance your sexual performance, but they don't work for me. Maybe I put them on too soon.

GARRY SHANDLING

We keep fighting about sex and money. I mean, she charges me so much, you know.

RODNEY DANGERFIELD

The sexes are so different. Women go out and say, "Before I go to bed with a man, I want to know who he is as a person." Guys are thinking, "Let's get them in bed before they find out who we are."

TONY STONE

A psychiatrist asks a lot of expensive questions that your wife asks for nothing.

JOEY ADAMS

The only thing that holds a marriage together is the husband being big enough to step back and see where the wife is wrong.

ARCHIE BUNKER

Our great flaw is our inability to commit. We see women: "Yes, I will love her and devote my life to her forever and . . . wait . . . there goes another one!"

BRAD STINE

Money

Rich

Money is better than poverty, if only for financial reasons.

WOODY ALLEN

A man who has a million dollars is as well off as if he were rich.

JOHN JACOB ASTOR

640K ought to be enough for anybody.

BILL GATES

What's a thousand dollars? Mere chicken feed.
A poultry matter.

GROUCHO MARX

I believe that the power to make money is a gift
from God.

JOHN D. ROCKEFELLER

Somebody said to me, "But the Beatles were
antimaterialistic." That's a huge myth. John and I
literally used to sit down and say, "Now, let's write a
swimming pool."

PAUL MCCARTNEY

Seek wealth, it's good.

IVAN BOESKY

There is nothing wrong with men possessing riches,
but the wrong comes when riches possess men.

BILLY GRAHAM

I'd like to live like a poor man with lots of money.

PABLO PICASSO

I'm opposed to millionaires, but it would be
dangerous to offer me the position.

MARK TWAIN

It isn't necessary to be rich and famous to be happy. It's only necessary to be rich.

ALAN ALDA

Money isn't everything as long as you have enough.

MALCOLM FORBES

There must be more to life than having everything.

MAURICE SENDAK

People think we make $3 million and $4 million a year. They don't realize that most of us only make $500,000.

PETE INCAVIGLIA

If I weren't earning $3 million a year to dunk a basketball, most people on the street would run in the other direction if they saw me coming.

CHARLES BARKLEY

My family got all over me because they said Bush is only for the rich people. Then I reminded them, "Hey, I'm rich."

CHARLES BARKLEY

I am not rich. I am a poor man with money, which is not the same thing.

GABRIEL GARCÍA MARQUEZ

Those people were so rich they had a Persian rug made out of real Persians.

HENNY YOUNGMAN

I'm convinced that certain facts of life are disguised by the powers that be to keep poor people from seeing how much fun it is to be rich. I mean, I've been broke and I've had money, and it's a lot of fun having money.

JAY LENO

It is better to be rich and healthy than poor and sick.

DAVE BARRY

POOR

I started out with nothing. I still have most of it.

MICHAEL DAVIS

Look at me: I worked my way up from nothing to a state of extreme poverty.

GROUCHO MARX

There were times my pants were so thin I could sit on a dime and tell if it was heads or tails.

SPENCER TRACY

Lack of money is the root of all evil.

GEORGE BERNARD SHAW

There was a time when a fool and his money were soon parted, but now it happens to everybody.

ADLAI STEVENSON

I've got all the money I'll ever need if I die by four o'clock.

HENNY YOUNGMAN

We had so little to eat that when Mom would throw a bone to the dog, he'd have to call for a fair catch.

LEE TREVINO

Poor people have more fun than rich people, they say; and I notice it's the rich people who keep saying it.

JACK PAAR

The trouble with being poor is that it takes up all of your time.

WILLEM DE KOONING

The trouble with unemployment is that the minute you wake up in the morning you're on the job.

SLAPPY WHITE

Times have sure changed. Yesterday a bum asked me if I could spare $2.75 for a double cappuccino with no foam.

BILL JONES

When I approached the checkout counter of a Miami store, the clerk said, "Cash, check, or stickup?"

PAT WILLIAMS

Money is the poor people's credit card.

MARSHALL MCLUHAN

I come from New York, where if you fall down someone will pick you up by your wallet.

AL MCGUIRE

When people ask me if I have any spare change, I tell them I have it at home in my spare wallet.

NICK ARNETTE

Everyone should have a roof over their head. If you also want walls and a floor, you may be getting out of your price range.

GENE PERRET

I used to think I was poor. Then they told me I wasn't poor, I was needy. Then they told me it was self-defeating to think of myself as needy. I was deprived. Then they told me that underprivileged was overused. I was disadvantaged. I still don't have a dime. But I have a great vocabulary.

JULES FEIFFER

He couldn't even afford to buy his little boy a yo-yo for Christmas. He just managed to get him a yo.

MAX KAUFFMANN

MAKING IT

The safest way to double your money is to fold it over once and put it in your pocket.

KIN HUBBARD

Buy low, sell high, collect early, and pay late.

DICK LEVIN

If at first you don't succeed, you may be at your level of incompetence already.

LAURENCE J. PETER

If at first you don't succeed, try, try again. Then quit.
No use being a damn fool about it.

W.C. FIELDS

The usual drawback to success is that it annoys one's
friends so.

P.G. WODEHOUSE

In the business world, everyone is paid in two coins:
cash and experience. Take the experience first; the
cash will come later.

HAROLD GENEEN

Choose a job you love and you will never have to
work a day in your life.

CONFUCIUS

Two teenage boys were counterfeiting money. One friend said to the other, "Where can we spend these fake thirty-five-dollar bills?" His friend said, "Let's take them to Charlie's Liquor Store. He's a dense old man." When they got to Charlie's, they handed him one of the bogus bills and asked him, "Can you change a thirty-five dollar bill?" He put it in his cash register and told them, "Not a problem." Then he handed them a bunch of cash, and the boys' eyes lit up. When they got outside, they noticed that Charlie had given them five sevens.

ADAM CHRISTING

You can marry more money in five minutes than you can earn in a lifetime.

BRECK SPEED AND MARK DUTTON

After a certain point money is meaningless. It ceases to be the goal. The game is what counts.

ARISTOTLE ONASSIS

BUSINESS

Business is a combination of war and sport.

ANDRÉ MAUROIS

The secret in business is to know something that nobody else knows.

ARISTOTLE ONASSIS

Business? It's quite simple—it's other people's money.

ALEXANDRE DUMAS

Any business arrangement that is not profitable to the other fellow will in the end prove unprofitable for you. The bargain that yields mutual satisfaction is the only one that is apt to be repeated.

B.C. FORBES

Experience teaches you that the man who looks
you straight in the eye, particularly if he adds a firm
handshake, is hiding something.

CLIFTON FADIMAN

The darkest hour of any man's life is when he sits
down to plan how to get money without earning it.

HORACE GREELEY

The salary of the chief executive of the large
corporation is not a market award for achievement.
It is frequently in the nature of a warm personal
gesture by the individual to himself.

JOHN KENNETH GALBRAITH

A verbal contract isn't worth the paper it's written on.

SAM GOLDWYN

If all economists were laid end to end, they would not reach a conclusion.

GEORGE BERNARD SHAW

The only function of economic forecasting is to make astrology look respectable.

EZRA SOLOMON

Nothing is illegal if a hundred businessmen decide to do it.

ANDREW YOUNG

I got a traffic ticket the other day so I went to see a lawyer who charges by the minute. When I asked him the first question he said, "Wwwwwwellllllll Mmmmmmmmisssssssssssster Aaaaaaaaaaarrrrrrrrrnnnnnnnnnneeeeeeette . . ."

NICK ARNETTE

McGowan's Madison Avenue Axiom: If an item is advertised as "under $50," you can bet it's not $19.95.

ARTHUR BLOCH

Now I'm in real trouble. First my laundry called and said they lost my shirt, and then my broker said the same thing.

LEOPOLD FECHTNER

I called my broker yesterday and he put me on hold. By the time he got back on the phone, I had nothing left to talk to him about.

GENE PERRET

October, this is one of the peculiarly dangerous months to speculate in stocks. The others are: July, January, September, April, November, May, March, June, December, August and February.

MARK TWAIN

Stock prices plunged sharply today as investors reacted to the discovery that Saturn actually has six moons rather than five, as was believed previously.

DAVE BARRY

Trading financial futures is only slightly more risky than feeding your cash directly to pigs.

BRECK SPEED AND MARK DUTTON

If it quacks like a duck, walks like a duck, and looks like a duck, most likely it is a junk bond.

BRECK SPEED AND MARK DUTTON

Buy land, they're not making it anymore.

MARK TWAIN

By working faithfully eight hours a day, you may eventually get to be boss and work twelve hours a day.

ROBERT FROST

The thing to do is to make so much money that you don't have to work after the age of twenty-seven. In case this is impracticable, stop work at the earliest possible moment, even if it is a quarter past eleven in the morning of the day when you find you have enough money.

ROBERT BENCHLEY

The question isn't at what age I want to retire—it's at what income.

GEORGE FOREMAN

My, my—sixty-five. I guess this marks the first day of the rest of my life savings.

H. MARTIN

[My job is] fun. But what's so unbelievable is that they are actually paying me money to have this much fun.

JAY LENO

I Owe, I Owe

If there's anyone listening to whom I owe money, I'm prepared to forget it if you are.

ERROL FLYNN

How can they say I'm bankrupt? I owe billions of dollars.

WILLIAM ZECKENDORF, SR.

Always live within your income, even if you have to borrow money to do so.

JOSH BILLINGS

With our first child, I must admit I wasn't prepared for the hospital sticker shock. My wife did all the work, but the hospital still charged us over $5,000. I couldn't afford that, so we had to put our daughter on layaway.

ROBERT G. LEE

Blessed are the young, for they shall inherit the national debt.

HERBERT HOOVER

I had a hard time at the bank today. I tried to take out a loan and they pulled a real attitude with me. Apparently, they won't accept the voices in my head as references.

STEVE ALTMAN

I had plastic surgery last week. I cut up my credit cards.

HENNY YOUNGMAN

I don't want money. It is only people who pay their bills who want that, and I never pay mine.

OSCAR WILDE

I'm living so far beyond my income that we may almost be said to be living apart.

E. E. CUMMINGS

"How did you go bankrupt?" Bill asked. "Two ways," Mike said. "Gradually and then suddenly."

ERNEST HEMINGWAY

I passed a car dealership. I looked in the window and I saw the most beautiful cars. And a fellow came out and said, "Come on in, they're bigger than ever and they last a lifetime!" He was talking about the payments.

CORBETT MONICA

Drive-in banks were established so most of the cars today could see their real owners.

E. JOSEPH COSSMAN

If you think nobody cares if you're alive, try missing a couple of car payments.

EARL WILSON

My brother's name is Greg, but when he got out of college he changed his name to Mkazi, which means "He who runs from student loan people."

TONY EDWARDS

A man must properly pay the fiddler. In my case it so happened that a whole symphony orchestra had to be subsidized.

JOHN BARRYMORE

An American is a person who yells for the government to balance the budget and borrows fifty dollars till payday.

H. ALAN DUNN

If all the nations in the world are in debt, where did all the money go?

STEVEN WRIGHT

GOVERNMENT

I owe the government $3,400 in taxes. So I sent them two hammers and a toilet seat.

MICHAEL MCSHANE

Next to being shot at and missed, nothing is really quite as satisfying as an income-tax refund.

F.J. RAYMOND

Income-tax returns are the most imaginative fiction being written today.

HERMAN WOUK

Income tax has made more liars out of the American people than golf has.

WILL ROGERS

I saw a bumper sticker on a Mercedes that said,
"I brake for tax shelters."

NICK ARNETTE

The taxpayer—that's someone who works for the
Federal government but doesn't have to take a civil-
service examination.

RONALD REAGAN

One of the things we have to be thankful for is that
we don't get as much government as we pay for.

CHARLES F. KETTERING

It is just as important that business keep out of
government as that government keep out of business.

HERBERT HOOVER

The key economic indicator of a recession is that government economists go around announcing that the economy is improving.

DAVE BARRY

Money is so strange these days. Get a computer and take six months to pay for it. Get a new car and take six years to pay for it. Get a new government program, and in just sixty years your grandchildren will have it paid off.

BILL JONES

We're a trillion dollars in debt. Who do we owe this money to? Someone named Vinnie?

ROBIN WILLIAMS

The government spends so much money. I've heard that they recently put a box on the counter of the Treasury Department that says, "Need a billion? Take a billion! Got a billion? Leave a billion!"

BILL JONES

VIRTUES AND VICES

Money doesn't always bring happiness. People with ten million dollars are no happier than people with nine million dollars.

HOBART BROWN

All right, so I like spending money! But name one other extravagance!

MAX KAUFFMANN

I withdrew my life savings from the bank. The teller asked, "How would you like that? Heads or tails?"

GENE PERRET

Part of the loot went for gambling, part for horses, and part for women. The rest I spent foolishly.

GEORGE RAFT

People look at me and say, "The guy has no regard for money." That is not true. I have had regard for money. There's some people who worship money as something you've got to have piled up in a big pile somewhere. I've only thought of money in one way— and that is to do something with.

WALT DISNEY

I know of nothing more despicable and pathetic than a man who devotes all the hours of the working day to the making of money for money's sake.

JOHN D. ROCKEFELLER

Old men are always advising young men to save money. That is bad advice. Don't save every nickel. Invest in yourself. I never saved a dollar until I was forty years old.

HENRY FORD

Nobody works as hard for his money as the man who marries it.

KIN HUBBARD

Mugger: "Your money or your life!" (pause)
Mugger: "Look, Bud, I said your money or your life!"
Jack Benny: "I'm thinking it over."

JACK BENNY

It is a gorgeous gold pocket watch. I'm proud of it.
My grandfather, on his deathbed, sold me this watch.

WOODY ALLEN

A man's gotta make at least one bet a day, else he
could be walking around lucky and never know it.

JIMMY JONES

I used to be a heavy gambler. But now I just make mental bets. That's how I lost my mind.

STEVE ALLEN

Money is like manure. If you spread it around it does a lot of good. But if you pile it up in one place, it stinks like hell.

CLINT MURCHISON, JR.

Carnegie exemplifies to me a truth about American money men that many earnest people fail to grasp—which is that the chase and the kill are as much fun as the prize, which you then proceed to give away.

ALISTAIR COOKE

Money's no good if you use it as a weapon. . . . If you share it, you'll always have enough. And if you don't, you'll never have enough.

CHI CHI RODRÍGUEZ

It's pretty hard to tell what does bring happiness; poverty and wealth have both failed.

KIN HUBBARD

It is a kind of spiritual snobbery that makes people think that they can be happy without money.

ALBERT CAMUS

Save a little money each month and at the end of the year you'll be surprised at how little you have.

ERNEST HASKINS

Saving is a very fine thing. Especially when your parents have done it for you.

WINSTON CHURCHILL

It is difficult to save money when your neighbors keep buying things you can't afford.

BRECK SPEED AND MARK DUTTON

I try to save my money. Who knows? Maybe one day it'll become valuable again.

MILTON BERLE

I don't like money. The minute I get it, I get rid of it!

NAZARETH

My wife makes the budget work. We do without a lot of things I don't need.

MILTON BERLE

Why do you think I'm fighting? The glory? The agony of defeat? You show me a man says he ain't fighting for money, I'll show you a fool.

LARRY HOLMES

They say that money talks, but the only thing it ever said to me was goodbye.

JOE LOUIS

I always throw my loose change into a large vase because my mother always told me "a penny saved is a penny urned."

GENE PERRET

And Finally

If you know how people feel about money, that's more revealing than any other single thing I know, including sleeping with them.

JERRY STERNER

I love everything about money. I love to *eat* it. Some people say you can't take it with you. I'm taking it with me.

STEVE MARTIN

I figure, you can't take it with you. You never see luggage tied on top of a hearse.

DAVID BRENNER

I don't like money actually, but it quiets my nerves.

JOE E. LEWIS

It frees you from doing things you dislike. Since I dislike doing nearly everything, money is handy.

GROUCHO MARX

Money doesn't buy friends, but it allows a better class of enemies.

LORD MANCROFT

Money often costs too much.

RALPH WALDO EMERSON

A nickel ain't worth a dime anymore.

YOGI BERRA

Inflation—that's when prices go from reasonable to expensive to "How much have you got with you?"

BOB HOPE

Money is God in action.

RAYMOND CHARLES BARKER

Money will come when you are doing the right thing.

MIKE PHILIPS

If a man is wise, he gets rich, an' if he gets rich, he gets foolish, or his wife does. That's what keeps money movin' around.

FINLEY PETER DUNNE

When I was young I thought money was the most important thing in life; now that I am old I know that it is.

OSCAR WILDE

Money is a singular thing. It ranks with love as man's greatest source of joy. And with death as his greatest source of anxiety. Money differs from an automobile, a mistress or cancer in being equally important to those who have it and those who do not.

JOHN KENNETH GALBRAITH

The dollar has become the single most powerful motivating factor in our society.

EDWARD JAMES OLMOS

Money is the only substance which can keep a cold world from nicknaming a citizen "Hey, you!"

WILSON MIZNER

A fool and his money were lucky to get together in the first place.

HARRY ANDERSON

Money's just a way of keeping score.

H. L. HUNT

SPORTS

GENERALLY SPEAKING

Sports is the toy department of human life.

HOWARD COSELL

Sports do not build character. They reveal it.

HEYWOOD HALE BROUN

In sport you either get tremendous fulfillment or tremendous disappointment. Nothing else in life is so cut and dried.

RICHARD MEADE

I always turn to the sports pages first, which record people's accomplishments. The front page has nothing but man's failures.

CHIEF JUSTICE EARL WARREN

Sports is the only entertainment where, no matter how many times you go back, you never know the ending.

NEIL SIMON

Serious sport has nothing to do with fair play. It is bound up with hatred, jealousy, boastfulness, disregard of all rules, and sadistic pleasure in witnessing violence: In other words, it is war minus the shooting.

GEORGE ORWELL

All pro athletes are bilingual. They speak English and profanity.

GORDIE HOWE

Jimmy Brown was the finest all-around athlete I ever saw: he was a jock of all trades.

JON WEBER

I was given the gifts to become not only an athlete but also a businessman, a thinker who could help dispel the myth that most athletes are dumb jocks who can't see beyond the next game.

EARVIN "MAGIC" JOHNSON

One man can be a crucial ingredient on a team, but one man cannot make a team.

KAREEM ABDUL-JABBAR

Coaching is like being king. It prepares you for nothing.

HERB BROOKS

Coaching is like running a restaurant. You cook one bad meal and everyone tells eight others about it. Cook a good meal and no one tells anyone.

PIERRE PAGE

Do you know what the best three years of a sports-writer's life are? Third grade.

GEORGE RAVELING

Losing streaks are funny. If you lose at the beginning, you got off to a bad start. If you lose in the middle of the season, you're in a slump. If you lose at the end, you're choking.

GENE MAUCH

The trouble with officials is they just don't care who wins.

TOMMY CANTERBURY

Wherever I go people are waving at me. Maybe if I do a good job, they'll use all their fingers.

FRANK KING

The Winter Olympics are easier [to host]. Nobody asks whether any of the bobsledders are going to arbitration.

TIM MCCARVER

Money is the driving force in college sports.
If NBC tells Notre Dame to kick off at 3, all they ask is A.M. or P.M.

BEANO COOK

If God had an agent, the world wouldn't be built yet. It'd only be about Thursday.

JERRY REYNOLDS

If we had ESPN twenty-two years ago, we'd have never had any kids.

TERRY TAUX

Sports is the only profession I know that when you retire, you have to go to work.

EARL MONROE

When you are not practicing, remember someone is practicing, and when you meet him, he will win.

ED MACAULEY

Sports serve society by providing vivid examples of excellence.

GEORGE F. WILL

Sport is a wonderfully democratic thing, one of the few honorable battlefields left. It is a conflict between good and bad, winning and losing, praise and criticism. Its true values should be treasured and protected . . . they belong to the people.

DANNY BLANCHFLOWER

BASEBALL

Baseball was, is, and always will be to me the best game in the world.

BABE RUTH

Baseball to me is still the national pastime because it is a summer game. I feel that almost all Americans are summer people, that summer is what they think of when they think of their childhood. I think it stirs up an incredible emotion in people.

STEVE BUSBY

What's important is that baseball, after twenty-eight years of artificial turf and expansion and the designated hitter and drugs and free agency and thousand-dollar bubble gum cards, is still a gift given by fathers to sons.

MICHAEL CHABON

Baseball is something more than a game to an American boy; it is his training field for life work. Destroy his faith in its squareness and honesty and you have destroyed something more; you have planted suspicion of all things in his heart.

JUDGE KENESAW MOUNTAIN LANDIS

You gotta be a man to play baseball for a living but you gotta have a lot of little boy in you, too.

ROY CAMPANELLA

You always get a special kick on opening day, no matter how many you go through. You look forward to it like a birthday party when you're a kid. You think something wonderful is going to happen.

JOE DIMAGGIO

Baseball is like church. Many attend. Few understand.

LEO DUROCHER

Statistics are to baseball what a flaky crust is to Mom's apple pie.

HARRY REASONER

Baseball is the only game you can see on the radio.

PHIL HERSH

The majority of American males put themselves to sleep by striking out the batting order of the New York Yankees.

JAMES THURBER

You don't need Little League. You don't even need nine kids. Four is plenty—a pitcher, a batter, and a couple shaggers. You can play ball all day long. My kids used to try to get me out there, but I'd just say, "Go play with your brothers." If kids want to do something, they'll do it. They don't need adults to do it for them.

YOGI BERRA

I bet you don't know what the first thing Little Leaguers always ask me: "How much money do you make?"

ROCKY BRIDGES

I'm not disloyal. I'm the most loyal player money can buy.

DON SUTTON

Under the circumstances, I wouldn't have the job [of baseball commissioner] today. It's impossible to do it. Every time the commissioner makes a decision, he's in court. Every player has an agent; every club owner has a lawyer. The game has left the field and gone to court.

HAPPY CHANDLER

Throwing people out of a game is like learning to ride a bike—once you get the hang of it, it can be a lot of fun.

RON LUCIANO

If they did get a machine to replace us [umpires], you know what would happen to it? Why, the players would bust it to pieces every time it ruled against them. They'd clobber it with a bat.

HARRY WENDELSTEDT

When I began playing the game, baseball was as gentlemanly as a kick in the crotch.

TY COBB

I could never play in New York. The first time I ever came into a game there, I got into the bullpen car and they told me to lock the door.

MIKE FLANAGAN

When I was a kid, I wanted to play baseball and join the circus. With the Yankees, I've been able to do both.

GRAIG NETTLES

There isn't enough mustard in the world to cover Reggie Jackson.

DAROLD KNOWLES

I am the best in baseball. . . . I create an excitement when I walk on the field.

REGGIE JACKSON

It ain't bragging if you can do it.

DIZZY DEAN

Police have arrested the man who was pictured throwing snowballs at Giants Stadium. If convicted, he [may] face six months in jail and a $1,000 fine. If it turns out he was under the influence of alcohol or drugs, he'll be signed by the Yankees.

DAVID LETTERMAN

I'm no different than anyone else with two arms, two legs, and forty-two-hundred hits.

PETE ROSE

I'll tell you how smart Pete [Rose] is. When they had the blackout in New York, he was stranded 13 hours on an escalator.

JOE NUXHALL

All baseball fans are provincial. They don't want the best team to win. They want their team to win.

ART HILL

The guy with the biggest stomach will be the first to take off his shirt at a baseball game.

GLENN DICKEY

If people don't want to come out to the ball park, nobody's going to stop them.

YOGI BERRA

Baseball is ninety percent mental. The other half
is physical.

YOGI BERRA

Our similarities are different.

DALE BERRA

I really didn't say everything I said.

YOGI BERRA

Pitching is the art of instilling fear.

SANDY KOUFAX

Nolan Ryan is pitching much better now that he has his curve ball straightened out.

JOE GARAGIOLA

Trying to throw a fastball by Hank Aaron is like trying to sneak the sun past a rooster.

CURT SIMMONS

I never threw an illegal pitch. The trouble is, once in a while I toss one that ain't never been seen by this generation.

SATCHEL PAIGE

I knew I was in trouble when they started clocking my fast ball with a sundial.

JOE MAGRANE

When the bullpen phone rings, we just jump up and run in circles. It's like musical chairs when the music ends—whoever doesn't have a seat will go in to pitch.

DAN QUISENBERRY

The secret of managing is to keep the guys who hate you away from the guys who are undecided.

CASEY STENGEL

I managed a team that was so bad, we considered a 2-and-0 count on the batter a rally.

RICH DONNELLY

I asked [my wife] how she would like to be married to a big-league manager, and she said, "You mean Tommy Lasorda is getting a divorce?"

JOHN WATHAN

There goes Rick Monday. He and Manny Mota are so old that they were waiters at the Last Supper.

TOMMY LASORDA

You can plant two thousand rows of corn with the fertilizer [Tommy] Lasorda spreads around.

JOE GARAGIOLA

I swing big, with everything I've got. I hit big or I miss big. I like to live as big as I can.

BABE RUTH

Swing at the strikes.

YOGI BERRA

When Neil Armstrong set foot on the moon, he found a baseball that Jimmy Foxx hit off me in 1937.

LEFTY GOMEZ

No one can ever see the ball hit the bat because it's physically impossible to focus your eyes that way. However, when I hit the ball especially hard, I could smell the leather start to burn as it struck the wooden bat.

TED WILLIAMS

[Stan Musial] could hit .300 with a fountain pen.

JOE GARAGIOLA

Charlie Gehringer is in a rut. He bats .350 on opening day and stays there all season.

LEFTY GOMEZ

You don't get your first home run too often.

RICK WRONA

The runners have returned to their respectable bases.

DIZZY DEAN

Never trust a base runner who's limping. Comes a base hit and you'll think he just got back from Lourdes.

JOE GARAGIOLA

Baseball players are the weirdest of all. I think it's all that organ music.

PETER GENT

Going to bed with a woman never hurt a ball player. It's staying up all night looking for them that does you in.

CASEY STENGEL

I can't understand why [catcher Joe Torre] hasn't been nicknamed Chicken. Don't you get it? "Chicken Catcher Torre."

BOBBY BRAGAN

Cool Papa Bell was so fast he could get out of bed, turn out the lights across the room, and be back in bed under the covers before the lights went out.

JOSH GIBSON

The doctors X-rayed my head and found nothing.

DIZZY DEAN

[Ted Simmons] didn't sound like a baseball player. He said things like "Nevertheless," and "If, in fact."

DAN QUISENBERRY

You have to have a certain dullness of mind and spirit to play here. I went through psychoanalysis, and that helped me deal with my Cubness.

JIM BROSNAN

Putting lights in Wrigley Field is like putting aluminum siding on the Sistine Chapel.

ROGER SIMON

All I remember about my wedding day in 1967 is that the Cubs lost a double-header.

GEORGE WILL

With the Cardinals I'd come in and find everyone reading the stock-market reports. With the Pirates, I come in and find everyone checking the papers to see if Hulk Hogan won.

ANDY VAN SLYKE

A hot dog at the ballpark is better than a steak at the Ritz.

HUMPHREY BOGART

If you're not having fun in baseball, you miss the point of everything.

CHRIS CHAMBLISS

There is always some kid who may be seeing me for the first or last time. I owe him my best.

JOE DIMAGGIO

The other sports are just sports. Baseball is a love.

BRYANT GUMBEL

Baseball is all clean lines and clear decisions. . . .
Wouldn't life be far easier if it consisted of a series of
definitive calls; safe or out, fair or foul, strike or ball.
Oh, for a life like that, where every day produces a
clear winner and an equally clear loser, and back to it
the next day with the slate wiped clean and the teams
starting out equal.

ERIC ROLFE GREENBERG

The bases were drunk and I painted the black with
my best yakker. But blue squeezed me, and I went
full. I came back with my heater, but the stick flares
one the other way and chalk flies for two bases. Three
earnies! Next thing I know, skipper hooks me and I'm
sipping suds with the clubby.

ED LYNCH

FISHING

Fishing is a chance to wash one's soul with pure air, with the rush of the brook, or with the shimmer of the sun on the blue water. . . . And it is discipline in the equality of man—for all men are equal before fish.

HERBERT HOOVER

Often, I have been exhausted on trout streams, uncomfortable, wet, cold, briar-scarred, sunburned, mosquito-bitten, but never, with a fly rod in my hand, have I been unhappy.

CHARLES KURALT

A fisherman is a lazy bad boy grown up. . . . He is dirty and disobedient, he plays hooky and won't work.

ZANE GREY

There were lots of people who committed crimes during the year who would not have done so if they had been fishing, and I assure you that the increase in crime is due to a lack of those qualities of mind and character which impregnate the soul of every fisherman except those who get no bites.

HERBERT HOOVER

You can always tell a fisherman, but you can't tell him much.

COREY FORD

Fishermen are born honest, but they get over it.

ED ZERN

The fishing was so good, I thought I was there yesterday.

DAVE ENGERBRETSON

Fisherman don't lie. They just tell beautiful stories.

SYNGMAN RHEE

Every man has a fish in his life that haunts him.

NEGLEY FARSON

There is no use in your walking five miles to fish when you can depend on being just as unsuccessful near home.

MARK TWAIN

There's a fine line between fishing and just standing on the shore like an idiot.

STEVEN WRIGHT

I watched a fishing show today on TV. Have you ever watched fishing for about 15 minutes and said, "Boy, I need a life"?

BRIAN REGAN

It doesn't matter if you catch any fish. What does matter is just being with yourself.

AL FIELDS

I have laid aside business, and gone a-fishing.

IZAAK WALTON

FOOTBALL

Some people think football is a matter of life and death. I can assure you it is much more important than that.

BILL SHANKLY

It's amazing what the human body can do when chased by a bigger human body.

JACK THOMPSON

Football doesn't build character. It eliminates the weak ones.

DARRELL ROYAL

Football is not a contact sport. It's a collision sport. Dancing is a good example of a contact sport.

DUFFY DAUGHERTY

Football features two of the worst aspects of American life—violence and committee meetings.

GEORGE WILL

Kicking is very important in football. In fact, some of the more enthusiastic players even kick the football occasionally.

ALFRED HITCHCOCK

When I played pro football, I never set out to hurt anybody deliberately . . . unless it was, you know, important, like a league game or something.

DICK BUTKUS

Whenever they gave [Dick Butkus] the game ball, he ate it.

ALEX HAWKINS

Now that I'm retired, I want to say that all defensive linemen are sissies.

DAN FOUTS

I've found that prayers work best when you have big players.

KNUTE ROCKNE

John Elway is the master of the inconceivable pass thrown to the unreachable spot.

PAT SUMMERALL

Paul Hornung was an impact player for the Packers. He was also an impact player to half the females in the USA.

MAX MCGEE

I would rather score a touchdown than make love to the prettiest girl in the United States.

PAUL HORNUNG

Franco Harris faked me out so bad one time that I got a 15-yard penalty for grabbing my own face mask.

D. D. LEWIS

[Gale Sayers] looks no different than any other runner when he's coming at you, but when he gets there, he's gone.

GEORGE DONNELLY

I knew [Rocket Ismail] was fast, but I never knew how fast until I saw him playing tennis by himself.

LOU HOLTZ

[Roy Green] has two speeds—here he comes and there he goes.

BARRY WILBORN

I talked to [Joe Theismann] briefly on the phone for an hour and a half.

TONY KORNHEISER

Dan [Dierdorf] and I had our ups and downs. Once we didn't speak for two weeks. I didn't think it was right to interrupt him.

BOB COSTAS

My wife calls me "Much Maligned." She thinks that's my first name. Every time she reads a story about me, that's always in front of my name.

CHRIS BAHR

[**M**arcus Allen] carries so many tacklers with him, he's listed in the Yellow Pages under "Public Transportation."

BOB HOPE

Playing middle linebacker is like walking through a lion's cage in a three-piece pork-chop suit.

CECIL JOHNSON

Cal quarterback Joe Kapp used to call audibles that were just obscenities directed at the other team.

GREG ENNIS

Coaches have to watch for what they don't want to see and listen for what they don't want to hear.

JOHN MADDEN

I don't hire anybody not brighter than I am. If they're not brighter than I am, I don't need them.

BEAR BRYANT

The definition of an atheist in Alabama is a person who doesn't believe in Bear Bryant.

WALLY BUTTS

There are three important things in life: family, religion, and the Green Bay Packers.

VINCE LOMBARDI

My biggest problems are defensive linemen and offensive alumni.

BO SCHEMBECHLER

Describing Don Shula as intense is like describing the universe as fairly large.

DAVE BARRY

[Tom Landry's] such a perfectionist that if he were married to Dolly Parton he'd expect her to cook.

DON MEREDITH

If you're a pro coach, NFL stands for *Not for Long*.

JERRY GLANVILLE

I hear Elvis is living now in Michigan or Minnesota. Well, we'd like him to come and be on our bench. We don't care how much he weighs.

JERRY GLANVILLE

I left because of illness and fatigue—the fans were sick and tired of me.

JOHN RALSTON

My athletes are always willing to accept my advice as long as it doesn't conflict with their views.

LOU HOLTZ

My players can wear their hair as long as they want and dress any way they want. That is, if they can afford to pay their own tuition, meals, and board.

EDDIE ROBINSON

We definitely will be improved this year. Last year we lost 10 games. This year we only scheduled nine.

RAY JENKINS

At Arkansas, they made a stamp to commemorate you; then, after last year, they had to stop making it because people were spitting on the wrong side.

LOU HOLTZ

San Francisco has always been my favorite booing city. I don't mean the people boo louder or longer, but there is a very special intimacy. When they boo you, you know they mean you. Music, that's what it is to me. One time in Kezar Stadium they gave me a standing boo.

GEORGE HALAS

Officials are the only guys who can rob you and then get a police escort out of the stadium.

RON BOLTON

You have to be respectful when arguing with an official. I usually say, "Sir, are we watching the same game?"

HOMER SMITH

It was a brain transplant. I got a sportswriter's brain so I would be sure I had one that hadn't been used.

NORM VAN BROCKLIN

What's the difference between a three-week-old puppy and a sportswriter? In six weeks, the puppy stops whining.

MIKE DITKA

Football is a game played with the arms, legs, and shoulders—but mostly from the neck up.

KNUTE ROCKNE

This isn't nuclear physics, it's a game. How smart do you really have to be?

TERRY BRADSHAW

I never graduated from the University of Iowa, but I was only there for two terms—Truman's and Eisenhower's.

ALEX KARRAS

Football is a wonderful way to get rid of aggressive-
ness without going to jail for it.

HEYWOOD HALE BROWN

[The Oakland Raiders] were the only team in history
whose team picture showed both a front and side view.

KEN STABLER

Professional sports are getting so violent. Next season
they're having Monday Night Drive-By Football.

BILL JONES

Football's a great life. Just think . . . they pay you
great money to eat well, stay in shape, and have fun.

HUGH MCELHENNY

There is an intensity and a danger in football—as in life generally—which keeps us alive and awake. It is a test of our awareness and ability. Like so much of life, it presents us with the choice of responding either with fear or action.

JOHN BRODIE

Boxing

A boxing match is like a cowboy movie. There's got to be good guys and there's got to be bad guys. That's what the people pay for, to see the bad guys get beat.

SONNY LISTON

Boxing is sort of like jazz. The better it is, the less amount of people can appreciate it.

GEORGE FOREMAN

I'm so fast I could hit you before God gets the news.

MUHAMMAD ALI

I believe in being gentle and knocking 'em out clean with a good punch on the right spot.

BOB FITZSIMMONS

Every man's got to figure to get beat sometime.

JOE LOUIS

When going into the ring I have always had it in mind that I would be the conqueror. That has always been my disposition.

JOHN L. SULLIVAN

I love boxing. Where else do two grown men prance around in satin underwear, fighting over a belt? . . . The one who wins gets a purse. They do it in gloves. It's the accessory connection I love.

JOHN MCGIVERN

My toughest fight was with my first wife.

MUHAMMAD ALI

The neighborhood where I grew up was so tough the
Avon Lady was Sonny Liston.

GEORGE RAVELING

Yes, I was fond of *les jeunes filles*. I liked to have a
new girl once a week when I was training for a fight.

GEORGES CARPENTER

Boxing is the best and most individual lifestyle you
can have in society without being a criminal.

RANDY NEUMANN

Sometimes Howard [Cosell] makes me wish I was a dog and he was a fireplug.

MUHAMMAD ALI

[Mike Tyson's] not all that bad. If you dig deep—dig real deep, dig, dig, dig, dig, dig deep, deep, go all the way to China—I'm sure you'll find there's a nice guy in there.

GEORGE FOREMAN

I know a lot of people think I'm dumb. Well, at least I ain't no educated fool.

LEON SPINKS

One day Don King will asphyxiate by the force of his own exhaust.

CARMEN GRACIANO

I was 6'1" when I started fighting, but with all the uppercuts I'm up to 6'5".

CHUCK WEPNER

There are more pleasant things to do than beat up people.

MUHAMMAD ALI

Hurting people is my business.

SUGAR RAY ROBINSON

You have to be able to get up off the floor when you can't.

JACK DEMPSEY

BASKETBALL

Michael Jordan goes up, stops for a cup of coffee, looks over the scenery, then follows through with a tomahawk jam.

BOB COUSY

In my prime I could have handled Michael Jordan. Of course, he would be only 12 years old.

JERRY SLOAN

I'm always mentioned in the same sentence as Michael Jordon: "You know that Scott Hastings; he's no Michael Jordon."

SCOTT HASTINGS

My biggest thrill came the night Elgin Baylor and I combined for 73 points in Madison Square Garden. Elgin had 71 of them.

HOT ROD HUNDLEY

You throw up an air ball and then Shaq goes up 15 feet to catch it and dunk it, and everyone say, "Wow, what a pass."

ANFERNEE HARDAWAY

Whatever [Dennis Rodman's] doing gets him 18 rebounds a game. I might have to paint my hair orange. He might be the normal one and all of us might be crazy. Ever think of that?

MALIK SEALY

You know what the key to good rebounding is? Being tall.

BILLY PACKER

You want to know the theory people play with today? Coaches tell the kids, "All five of you guys go ahead and foul at once, because they can only call one of 'em."

SONNY SMITH

We'll play [Notre Dame] anywhere we can get three good referees who aren't Catholic.

GENE KEADY

We don't need refs, but I guess the white guys need something to do. All the players are black.

CHARLES BARKLEY

If the Warren Commission were still active today, I'd send them a tape to determine whether one official acted alone or if there was a conspiracy.

GEORGE RAVELING

Bobby [Knight] is a good friend of mine. But if I ever need a heart transplant, I want his. It's never been used.

GEORGE RAVELING

I don't like all the time-outs. I run out of things to say to my team.

JIM VALVANO

A team should be an extension of a coach's personality. My teams were arrogant and obnoxious.

AL MCGUIRE

I like Frank Layden's autobiography—*Famous Men Who Have Known Me.*

PAT WILLIAMS

We had a booster club in Utah, but by the end of the season it had turned into a terrorist group.

FRANK LAYDEN

I told him, "Son, I can't understand it with you. Is it ignorance or apathy?" He said, "Coach, I don't know and I don't care."

FRANK LAYDEN

I asked [a recruit] to spell Mississippi. He said, "The state or the river?"

GEORGE RAVELING

I just can't recruit where there's grass around. You gotta have a concrete lawn before I feel comfortable enough to go in and talk to your parents.

AL MCGUIRE

I'll watch the kids play, have a big steak with my friends, stay in a nice hotel, sign autographs, then go back to Vegas and tell my alumni how tough recruiting is.

JERRY TARKANIAN

My intelligence is baffling. . . . If people ain't prepared for me, they may walk away knowing less than they did when they walked up.

EDGAR JONES

My whole family likes to play basketball. George II plays for his high school team and George III and George IV and George V are going to be good players. One day we're going to have a team and call it Georgetown.

GEORGE FOREMAN

One day of practice is like one day of clean living. It doesn't do you any good.

ABE LEMONS

If all I'm remembered for is being a good basketball player, then I've done a bad job with the rest of my life.

ISAIAH THOMAS

I don't think basketball is the answer to all problems. If a guy comes into the league with a ton of problems, and they pay him a million dollars, then he's a millionaire with a ton of problems.

KEVIN MCHALE

When we started, we used to make very little money and have a lot of fun. Now we make a lot of money and have no fun at all. I like it better this way.

ABE LEMONS

The Lakers are so good they could run a fast break with a medicine ball.

RICH DONNELLY

Last year [the Cavaliers] weren't all that bad. We led the league in flu shots.

BILL FITCH

This year we plan to run and shoot. Next year we plan to run and score.

BILLY TUBBS

[Basketball] is the second most exciting indoor sport, and the other one shouldn't have spectators.

DICK VERTLEIB

GOLF

When I get out on that green carpet called a fairway, manage to poke the ball right down the middle, my surroundings look like a touch of heaven on earth.

JIMMY DEMARET

Golf is like fishing and hunting. What counts is the companionship and fellowship of friends, not what you catch or shoot.

GEORGE ARCHER

Golf is the most fun you can have without taking your clothes off.

CHI CHI RODRÍGUEZ

Golf is a game with the soul of a 1956 Rotarian.

BILL MANDEL

Isn't it fun to go out on the course and lie in the sun?

BOB HOPE

I used to play golf with a guy who cheated so badly that he once had a hole in one and wrote down zero on his scorecard.

BOB BRUCE

Nobody but you and your caddie care what you do out there, and if your caddie is betting against you, he doesn't care either.

LEE TREVINO

Never bet with a man named "One-Iron."

TOM SHARP

If you are caught on a golf course during a storm and are afraid of lightning, hold up a 1-iron. Not even God can hit a 1-iron.

LEE TREVINO

The worst club in my bag is my brain.

CHRIS PERRY

I like golf because I can go out and hit a little white ball that doesn't move and doesn't hit back. It should be easy, but it isn't.

LAWRENCE TAYLOR

It took me 17 years to get 3,000 hits. I did it in one afternoon on the golf course.

HANK AARON

I was three over: one over a house, one over a patio, and one over a swimming pool.

GEORGE BRETT

My best score ever is 103. But I've only been playing 15 years.

ALEX KARRAS

[**Par** is] anything I want it to be. For instance, the hole right here is a par 47, and yesterday I birdied the sucker.

WILLIE NELSON

There are no pars, birdies, or bogeys—just numbers. Just string them together and add 'em up.

PETER JACOBSEN

This is a game of misses. The guy who misses the best is going to win.

BEN HOGAN

I expect to make at least seven mistakes a round. Therefore, when I make a bad shot, I don't worry about it. It's just one of those seven.

WALTER HAGEN

Golf is a game of days, and I can beat almost anyone on my day.

FUZZY ZOELLER

The more I practice, the luckier I get.

JERRY BARBER

You drive for show, but putt for dough.

BOBBY LOCKE

I never pray to God to make a putt. I pray to God to help me react good if I miss a putt.

CHI CHI RODRÍGUEZ

Ninety percent of the putts that fall short don't go in.

YOGI BERRA

The least thing upsets him on the links. He misses short putts because of the uproar of the butterflies in the adjoining meadows.

P. G. WODEHOUSE

As far as swing and techniques are concerned, I don't know diddly-squat. When I'm playing well, I don't even take aim.

FRED COUPLES

The ideal build for a golfer would be strong hands, big forearms, thin neck, big thighs, and a flat chest. He'd look like Popeye.

GARY PLAYER

The uglier a man's legs are, the better he plays golf. It's almost a law.

H.G. WELLS

My swing is so bad I look like a caveman killing his lunch.

LEE TREVINO

The point is that it doesn't matter if you look like a beast before or after the hit, as long as you look like a beauty at the moment of impact.

SEVE BALLESTEROS

The golf swing is like sex: You can't be thinking of the mechanics of the act while you're doing it.

DAVE HILL

Golf and sex are about the only things you can enjoy without being good at it.

JIMMY DEMARET

Golf is like love—one day you think you're too old, and the next you can't wait to do it again.

ROBERTO DEVICENZO

Jim was just beginning to make a putt when a funeral procession drove by the golf course. He bowed his head, holding his hat over his heart until the procession had passed, then he began putting again. His golf buddies said, "Wow, Jim, we had no idea you were a religious person. . . . That was very sensitive!" He replied, "Well, after all, I was married to her for twenty-eight years."

PETE MCLEOD

Give me my golf clubs, fresh air and a beautiful partner, and you can keep my golf clubs and the fresh air.

JACK BENNY

We have 51 golf courses in Palm Springs. [President Ford] never decides which one he will play until after his first tee shot.

BOB HOPE

If you think it's hard to meet new people, try picking up the wrong golf ball.

JACK LEMMON

For most players, golf is about as serene as a night in Dracula's castle.

JIM MURRY

They call it golf because all the other four-letter words were taken.

RAYMOND FLOYD

The great thing about golf—and this is the reason why a lot of health experts like me recommend it— you can drink beer and ride in a cart while you play.

DAVE BARRY

The first time I played the Masters, I was so nervous I drank a bottle of rum before I teed off. I shot the happiest 83 of my life.

CHI CHI RODRÍGUEZ

It doesn't matter how many Open championships or titles you may have won. When you stand on the tee at a Ryder Cup match and play for your country, your stomach rumbles like a kid turning up for his first tournament.

ARNOLD PALMER

The fans would like to see Palmer win, but they don't really care. They just want to see him. There never has been a guy who has done as much for sports as Arnie has for golf.

TOM WATSON

Some of us worship in churches, some in synagogues, some on golf courses.

ADLAI STEVENSON

HOCKEY

We know that hockey is where we live, where we can best meet and overcome pain and wrong and death. Life is just a place we spend time between games.

FRED SHERO

When Gordie [Howe] came into the NHL, hockey was a Canadian game. He converted it into a North American game.

CLARENCE CAMPBELL

I've got Americans. I've got Canadians. I've got Finns and Swedes and Czechs. If I ever get fired, I can always get a job at the United Nations.

HERB BROOKS

I went to a fight the other night, and a hockey game broke out.

RODNEY DANGERFIELD

We get nose jobs all the time in the NHL, and we don't even have to go to the hospital.

BRAD PARK

The fans love the fighting. The players don't mind. The coaches like the fights. What's the big deal?

DON CHERRY

A good fighting club will beat a club that has super-stars on it every time.

PUNCH IMLACH

If we don't put a stop to [the fighting], we'll have to start printing more tickets.

CONN SMYTHE

Everyone cheats in hockey. It's unbelievable how much you can get away with if you do it when no one is looking, or cares.

TOM LYSIAK

My career started slowly and then tapered off.

GARY MCCORD

When I was a kid, I used to pray to the Lord to make me a hockey player. I forgot to mention the NHL, and so I spent 16 years in the minors.

DON CHERRY

Goal tending is a normal job. Sure! How would you like it in your job if every time you made a small mistake, a red light went on over your desk and 15,000 people stood up and yelled at you.

JACQUES PLANTE

I have no sympathy for goalies. No sympathy at all.

MARIO LEMIEUX

It may sound strange, but the sign of a good hockey team is garbage goals.

BRIAN BURKE

He who lives by the cheap shot dies by the cross-check.

STAN FISCHLER

I skate to where the puck is going to be, not where it has been.

WAYNE GRETZKY

He [Rocket Richard] could find a loose puck in a pile of coal during a blackout.

WILLIAM LEGGETT

They called him Bobby [Orr], B.O., The Kid, or No. 4. For what he meant to us, they should have called him God.

DAN CANNEY

The New York Rangers are celebrating their victory by traveling around the city carrying the Stanley Cup. And out of habit, many New Yorkers are throwing change in it.

CONAN O'BRIEN

Teams that win drive to the rink at 60 or 65 mph because they're excited to get there. Teams that lose take their time. There's no rush. They go about 30 mph.

CHICO RESCH

You don't have to be crazy to play hockey, but it helps.

BOB PLAGER

You're not really a hockey player until you've lost a few teeth.

BILL GADSBY

MORE SPORTS

One of the advantages bowling has over golf is that you seldom lose a bowling ball.

DON CARTER

Climbing would be a great, truly wonderful thing if it weren't for all that damn climbing.

JOHN OHRENSCHALL

If God didn't want man to hunt, he wouldn't have given us plaid shirts.

JOHNNY CARSON

I went hunting for the first time. I shot an elk. I felt bad at first, but the guy was wearing a plaid leisure suit so he pretty much had it coming.

BRIAN KILEY

I only kill in self-defense. What would you do if a rabbit pulled a knife on you?

JOHNNY CARSON

The people I see on bicycles look like organic-gardening zealots who advocate Federal regulation of bedtime and want American foreign policy to be dictated by UNICEF. These people should be confined.

P.J. O'ROURKE

I see a lot of bicycles with baby seats on the back. Is this really fun for the kid? Dad's enjoying the fresh air and sunshine. Junior's got his nose wedged between sweaty butt cheeks all afternoon.

JONATHAN DROLL

I've always loved the luge. There is no sport that manages to be as ceaselessly similar from one competition to the next.

KEITH OLBERMANN

One day you just look up and you say, "Holy smoke, I never noticed that thing before." And then you discover it's a mourning dove, a really beautiful bird. Then you start chasing them, and before you know it you're collecting them. It's a grown-up version of a little boy's attempt to collect every baseball card. It becomes a kind of hunting game in which you begin to notice the beautiful things around you. And it gets you away from the humdrum of daily life. It's an obsession: I know a lot of birders who divorced non-birders and then married birders. You have to organize your life around birding, including your wife, or other-wise your new wife will think you're as nuts as your old one did.

JOHN LEO

I spent 12 years training for a career that was over in a week.

BRUCE JENNER

They thought la crosse was what you find in la church.

ROBIN WILLIAMS

I had this great idea to make the great wall of China into a handball court.

GEORGE GOBEL

If at first you don't succeed, I'd stay away from skydiving.

MILTON BERLE

When I realized that what I had turned out to be was a lousy, two-bit pool hustler and drunk, I wasn't depressed at all. I was glad to have a profession.

DANNY MCGOORTY

Driving a race car is like dancing with a chain saw.

CALE YARBOROUGH

When I first started racing, you didn't dare bring your wife or girlfriend to the race, because half the people were drunk and the rest were fighting.

RICHARD PETTY

And so in my sophomore year I went out for track, because track was the sport where you were least likely to have something thrown at you or have somebody run into you at high speed.

DAVE BARRY

Joggers should run in a wheel—like hamsters— because *I* don't want to look at them.

JOHN WATERS

Skiing combines outdoor fun with knocking down trees with your face.

DAVE BARRY

The sport of skiing consists of wearing three thousand dollars' worth of clothes and equipment and driving two hundred miles in the snow in order to stand around a bar and get drunk.

P. J. O'ROURKE

Cross-country skiing is great if you live in a small country.

STEVEN WRIGHT

If Borg's parents hadn't liked the name, he might never have been Bjorn.

MARTY INDIK

I don't know what it is, but I can't look at Hulk
Hogan and believe that he's the end result of millions
and millions of years of evolution.

JIM MURRAY

Winning and Losing

When you win, nothing hurts.

JOE NAMATH

There is no room for second place. There is only one
place in my game and that is first place.

VINCE LOMBARDI

Win any way you can as long as you can get away
with it.

LEO DUROCHER

It's not whether you win or lose—but whether *I* win or lose.

SANDY LYLE

The only time close counts is in horseshoes and dancing.

FRED HANEY

I don't think we can win every game. Just the next one.

LOU HOLTZ

For when the One Great Scorer comes to mark against your name,

He writes—not that you won or lost—but how you played the game.

GRANTLAND RICE

"How you play the game" is for college boys. When you're playing for money, winning is the only thing that counts.

LEO DUROCHER

There is too much emphasis on success and failure, and too little on how a person grows as he works. Enjoy the journey, enjoy every moment, and quit worrying about winning and losing.

MATT BIONDI

I hate to lose more than I love to win. I hate to see the happiness in their faces when they beat me.

JIMMY CONNORS

There are two sorts of losers—the good loser, and the one who can't act.

LAURENCE J. PETER

It's not whether you win or lose, but who gets
the blame.

BLAINE NYE

Winning isn't everything, but making the effort
to win is.

VINCE LOMBARDI

When you win, you eat better, sleep better, and
your beer tastes better. And your wife looks like
Gina Lollobrigida.

JOHNNY PESKY

You're a hero when you win and a bum when you lose.
That's the game.

JOHNNY UNITAS

Library of Congress Cataloging-in-Publication Data

Sex, money, & sports : quotations on the only things men talk about /
    compiled by Michael Maggio.
        p.   cm.
    ISBN 0-7352-0053-X (cloth)
    1. Sex—Quotations, maxims, etc.   2. Money—Quotations, maxims, etc.
3. Sports—Quotations, maxims, etc.   I. Maggio, Michael.   II. Title: Sex,
money, and sports.
PN6084.S49S495   1998
081—dc21   98-26087
                                                   CIP

Printed in the United States of America.

10 9 8 7 6 5 4 3 2 1

ISBN 0-7352-0053-X

Text design: *Tom Nery*

PRENTICE HALL PRESS
Paramus, NJ 07652

A Simon & Schuster Company

On the World Wide Web at http://www.phdirect.com

Prentice Hall International (UK) Limited, *London*
Prentice Hall of Australia Pty. Limited, *Sydney*
Prentice Hall of Canada, Inc., *Toronto*
Prentice Hall Hispanoamericana, S.A., *Mexico*
Prentice Hall of India Private Limited, *New Delhi*
Prentice Hall of Japan, Inc., *Tokyo*
Simon & Schuster Asia Pte. Ltd., *Singapore*
Editora Prentice Hall do Brasil, Ltda., *Rio de Janeiro*